TORONTO THE GOOD

By
Gerald Utting

An Album
of Colonial Hogtown

Devised and designed by Roland Morgan

Bodima Books

ISBN 0-88875-001-3

Typeset in Palatino face on Mergenthaler
Linoterm by Golden Temple Graphics. Printed
in Canada.
Cover design Roland Morgan & Bob Masse.

Bodima Books

BOX 48913, BENTALL CENTRE 3, VANCOUVER V7V 1A8

DISTRIBUTED BY
The Macmillan Company of Canada Limited
70 BOND STREET, TORONTO 2, ONTARIO, CANADA

INDEX

It was Sunday in 1899. The awful gloom of the Sabbath had settled down for 24 hours on Toronto. The citizens had decorated their door nails with crepe in honor of the austerity and solemnity of the day. The children, dressed in sombre colors, wended their way silently from Sunday school. The Island ferries were tied up. The Sunday band concerts had long been interdicted. The Sunday street cars had not operated for six months. In the Union Station yards a train load of cattle sweltered and thirsted in the burning sun. Itwas not lawful for anyone to give them water. At the corner of King and Yonge streets a rank growth of grass had forced itself between the scoria blocks. The rails were encrusted with moss and lichens.

Three men drove in a hired cab through the streets. It was the only vehicle in sight. The noise of the wheels reverberated like thunder along the empty vestas.

"At last," said S.H. Blake, "I am almost happy. Everybody else is so miserable."

"Yes," said another gentleman named Paterson, "things are coming our way. I was instrumental in having ten icemen executed yesterday for delivering their wares on Sunday. I have had one hundred milkmen arrested for violation of the Lord's Day Act. How shall we punish them, Brother Blake?"

"Hah," said the great Q.C., "we'll make them drink their own milk. By this time it will have turned sour. But those editors, Brother Paterson – those editors who published theatre notices, we'll hang them. We must stamp out this Satanic press."

"Still," volunteered Mr. O'Meara, "the town is hardly dead enough yet. I am agitating to make the street railway paint the trolleys black and toll the gongs. There is nothing like impressing on the people that in the midst of life we are in death."

"Did you hear," asked Mr. Paterson indignantly, "that a small boy was seen in High Park today?"

"The miscreant!" yelled Mr. Blake. "What will these worms do next? When we hve legislation to prevent even the brooks babbling on Sunday, will a small boy set us at naught?"

"Too true, Brother Blake."

"Well, then, I have a scheme. We will set cannon at every entrance to High Park. These will be operated by electric springs which no intruder can avoid stepping upon. Then the miserable creature will be blown to the place where every day is Sunday."

"Wonderful! Wonderful!" chimed his companions in chorus. "You are indeed a philanthropist! But when are you going to restrict the people to four breaths an hour on Sunday?"

At this juncture the dialogue ended. The cab, rickety from disuse, collapsed, and the three occupants were thrown to the ground. They were stunned. They spent the remainder of the Sabbath on the pavement. It was not lawful to remove them. **The Star Jan. 11th, 1898**

FOREWORD

The photographs in this book come from the Canadian History archives of the Metropolitan Toronto central library on Yonge Street, just above Bloor. This new building typifies in itself some of the things about Toronto that this book is intended to display.

For example, in 40 years' time, someone going into the by-then aging structure might ask himself (or herself): What stood here before the library was built? Who was the architect? Where did the previous buildings fit into the stream of Toronto life, and was that stream very much different from the world of 2020 AD? (This assumes there will be a world in those days.)

At the time of writing, I live in an apartment building on the next block to the new Metropolitan Library. I lived in the same building several years ago, then was suddenly shifted to Vancouver by my employer for a year. When I came back, there suddenly was this giant building standing where before there had been a construction site. I tried to remember what had been there before the construction site, but couldn't.

In the life of Toronto, this kind of thing has been going on for almost two centuries. Fortunately, photography was invented only a few decades after Toronto was established and we have more than a century of photographic records to give us visual impressions of what the city was like and how its people lived.

You can construct some kind of history of a city by poring through records of customs house clearances, transportation statistics, journals of political debates, even visit the few old houses that remain as museums, and go to such recreations as Pioneer Village, north of Toronto. But the best way I know of recapturing some of the spirit of the times is to look at photographs of people and buildings taken in the past. The cluttered but comfortable Victorian interiors do more than hint at the solid wealth of Toronto of 80 or 90 years ago–they display it. When you see the lavish padding of chairs and settees, the bric-a-brac scattered throughout the rooms, you are less surprised at the perhaps provincial, but very real, attempts at opulent display on the faces of many of those vanished buildings.

The statistics of the time cannot quite do it, but the photographs can capture the imagination one hundred years afterward. Look at the crowd scenes. There were a lot of people in Toronto even a century ago. They built the city, they are buried in its old cemeteries, which we have respected a lot more than we respected the buildings they worked in and the homes they lived in.

Now let me make a confession. I came to Toronto from the South Pacific in 1960, and I was stunned by its lack of charm, and its lack of fine buildings. The Old City Hall was grim and dark then, as was Queen's Park.

Witnesses Swear Island Hotel Sold Liquor Sunday – The Charges Dismissed By The Magistrate – City Bonifaces Fined For Selling After Hours – Charles Tilly, head bartender at the newly licensed hotel at Hanlan's Point was before the Magistrate today on two charges of selling liquor last Sunday, to which he pleaded not guilty.

Two informers, one of them vice-president of the Metropolitan Musical and Athletic Gambling Club, recently broken up by police, swore they bought lager beer in the barroom on Sunday, where they found a crowd drinking.

Tilly, his son Fred Thomas, resident manager and Joe Popp, special constable, all swore that no liquor was sold and that the licensed premises were hermetically sealed during Sunday afternoon. **The Star July 11th, 1895**

In the pictures in this book you will see many fine old buildings. Only a handful of them remain. For some reason, whether from commercial cupidity or lack of fire precautions, acres of old Toronto **were** wiped out as thoroughly as if bombed.

The fine old Toronto Star building, at 80 King Street West, once the highest in the Commonwealth, was standing when I went on an overseas assignment for The Star a few years ago. The Star had already shifted to the waterfront. When I came back, I was amazed, while strolling along King Street, to find there was just a big hole in the ground at 80 King West. Today there is an 80-storey skyscraper.

I am not against development of a city. The history of the world is one of change. Everything decays. But in Toronto there seems to have been in the past a remarkable zeal for destroying the finest buildings.

There are acres of horrible old warehouses dating from the 1890s and early 1900s that seem to resist all change, while mansions and temples of commerce from the late 19th century were smashed into rubble.

Perhaps there is a lesson for us. I hope this book will give some readers cause to think.

Other cities have immeasurably longer histories than Toronto. All of them face the problem of development. Some of them have managed to do better than others. Toronto has been doing better than most in recent years, but then we had already erased a very good part of the city's treasure trove of public and private architecture.

Yet I think of cities in Germany, great centres of industrial production, which have had to rebuild from the rubble of World War II and have been able to do so without destroying the visual links with their past. With any luck, some who look at the photographs in this book may be inspired to make sure that the heritage we are in the process of creating for our children and grandchildren in the New Toronto of the second half of the Twentieth Century will be of a quality that they will not lightly wish to destroy, and that what we can do in shaping their

A number of youthful horsemen are in the habit of frequenting the Queen's Park in the mornings and indulging in some rapid riding. Some of them are not particular about keeping to the beaten track, but gallop about in all directions, tearing up the turf as they go. No one would care to interfere with the amusement of these equestrians, but it should be some one's duty to see that the turf in the Park is not cut to pieces. Those who should look after the Park themselves need looking after. A short time ago attention was called repeatedly to the fact that cows were allowed to pasture in the Park, to the great discomfort of those who cared to ramble there, but no attention was paid to the matter. Perhaps the authorities take the view that the Park proper is now so limited in extent that it is not worth looking after. But many citizens take an entirely opposite view of the situation, and hold that as the Park is now very much reduced in size there is the greater need for looking well after what is left. **Globe & Mail Nov. 3rd, 1904**

outlook will also engender in them a feeling that the handiwork of their grandparents should not be so casually bashed down as has happened in our own past.

There was a move in the 1960s and early 1970s to destroy the Old City Hall, as the Armouries on University Avenue had been razed. It was defeated, but only just. Today, with the cleaning of this not-so-old building, the citizenry can admire its robust outlines and warm coloring, and sense a feeling of continuity. Yet it could easily have gone the other way. I had never seen the Old City Hall clean until a few years ago and had tended to think of it as a massive piece of black ugliness.

St. James Cathedral is a light and airy building today, but when I first saw it, it was dim and drab, with decades of soot grimed into it.

Queen's Park similarly has become one of the finest looking buildings in the city, following the removal of tons of soot.

Why did the citizens permit these structures to become so horrifyingly dirty? I have no answer. But there can be little doubt that this lack of civic spirit endangered every one of our public monuments.

Now the pictures in this book are not meant to be in themselves complete descriptions of anything. The past of Toronto is captured on film, in drawings, in books, documents, maps, and in the existing buildings of the city.

This is not a work for architects or historians to pick to pieces. It is rather something to whet the appetite of the reader, to go visit the galleries, in fact, to do those things which enable you to enjoy more the life you are living today. That, I suppose, is the greatest heritage any one can have–a total environment in which a human being can feel at ease, challenged, or anything he really wants to be.

Our National Spirit – For a cold and severely practical people, such as Canadians are generally reputed to be, especially among foreigners who do not know us, we are certainly doing fairly well these days, in the way of hero worship.

The unveiling of statues to our national heroes and statesmen seems to be the order of the day. While the memory of Sir John A. Macdonald is being perpetuated at Ottawa, Maisonneuve is also being similarly honored in Montreal, and still there are more to come, for the list of dead heroes is not yet exhausted.

While reviewing the past, the future also engages our attention, and the purely sentimental question of the most fitting emblazonment of our national flag is also exciting the people to an unwonted degree.

All this is as it should be, and let no one, at home or abroad, imagine that Canadians are frozen against these human feelings and emotions which go to make great nations. **The Star July 2nd, 1895**

POMP AND CIRCUMSTANCE

Toronto's long love affair with the pomp and circumstance of government–perhaps out of step in the new-nihilism of the late 1960s and early 1970s–came naturally. Though there had been trading posts on the site of Toronto since 1720, the real impetus for a permanent and significant British settlement at York came from John Graves Simcoe, first lieutenant governor of the newly-created Upper Canada. He wanted to create a military base that could be self-supporting economically as a bulwark to expansion by the recently independent American colonies.

Although there were better harbors on lake Ontario, Toronto was far enough away from the Americans to be relatively safe and close enough to serve as a base if hostilities should break out. "Toronto appears to be the natural arsenal of Lake Ontario," he wrote to the British government.

The British government went along with his plan, but parsimoniously, so that when the War of 1812 came, Fort York was important enough to be the target of an American amphibious assault, but not powerful enough to stop the invaders in their tracks. They burned down the village of York, in return for which the British burned down Washington. This was a source of great satisfaction to later generations of Torontonians, but perhaps the burned-out settlers of 1812 would have preferred to be let alone.

York became the captial of Upper Canada in 1793, at a time when it scarcely had any people at all, so it is fairly obvious that the business of the original settlement was government. The first wooden Parliament Building went up at what is now Front and Berkeley in 1796. The Americans burned them down. In 1818, a new Parliament was built of brick in the same place. It burned down more peacefully and a third Parliament was built near Simcoe Street. The big shift uptown came in 1893, when the present Ontario Legislature at Queen's Park was opened.

Kingston was the economic giant of Ontario for much of the early part of the nineteenth century. York's population in 1820 was only 1,240.

But Kingston was very much a satellite of Montreal, which already was a great city. The government of Upper Canada favored Toronto, and government was a growth industry almost as much then as now.

Beware Of Damage Claims – Like many other donations to the city, the gift of money toward the erection of a public lavatory threatens to be a white elephant for a time at least. All admit the desirability of such a convenience, yet no one wants it located alongside his property, and wherever the site may be chosen it is probable that protest will be made. An advertisement for a central property owner willing to have the lavatory close by his building would scarcely meet with an embarrassing number of replies.

The aldermen will be wise to make haste slowly. The city wants no more damage suits, and it would be well, before definitely selecting a site and starting work, to secure an agreement from all surrounding property owners and occupants promising not to claim damages. **The Star July 5th, 1894**

The road system, shipping, all began to depend on Toronto, and the ''better quality'' folk began to settle in York, to be able to rub shoulders with the lieutenant-governor and his staff.

The growth of the United States also impelled Toronto, which is within 500 miles of two thirds of the population of the U.S. And the railway enabled goods to be brought to Toronto from the port of New York just as rapidly as to Montreal, for there were no icebreakers on the St. Lawrence in those days.

Immigration played as big a part in the growth of Toronto during the Nineteenth Century as it has since World War II, though because most of the earlier immigrants were British this is sometimes forgotten.

Toronto was the capital of Canada West, the centre which launched the exploitation of the prairies. It saw itself as the main city of the British Empire, and Ontario provided its vice-regal representatives with a mansion right in the hub of the city, at King and Simcoe.

By the turn of the century, the lieutenant-governor's role had become largely ritualistic, because Toronto had become a commercial empire rather than a military one.

But they were very Loyal to the crown in those days–and most Torontonians probably still are, in a less fervid way–and balls at Government House and celebrations for visits by members of the Royal Family were treated as great occasions.

The pictures in the following chapter show the Government House that stood from 1868 to 1912, and the last dance in its ballroom.

For many years after that, Government House was Chorley Park in Rosedale, but the more democratic ambience of World War II turned it into a military hospital, then it was allowed to moulder away until it finally was torn down in the 1960s. Today, there is no Government House, but the lieutenant-governor receives guests in a suite at the Ontario Legislature.

But sessions of the legislature are still opened by parades that usually include plumed Horse Guards with silver cuirasses and lances.

Where skyscrapers now loom, this bastion of empire stood at King and Simcoe: Government House (1868-1912), pictured during the year it was pulled down.

In his citadel in 1912, the royal representative in Ontario, Sir John Morrison, the lieutenant-governor, overwhelms the camera with his courtly splendour.

Where sleep the great: Sir John Morrison's
bedroom in old Government House.

The wrecker's coming, so the stately couples of Toronto society have one last dance in the ballroom of old Government House: April 29, 1912.

After the ball was over: the old mansion came down in 1912, the new government house came down 50 years later. Today, the lieutenant-governor has a suite provided at the Ontario Legislature for ceremonies–and no ballroom.

This statue of the young Queen Victoria stood in Queen's Park in the 1870s. Today a statue of the great queen, but slightly older, stands right in front of the legislature.

15

Turn-of-the century prospect from
the balcony of the Legislature at
Queen's Park. Today we have
removed the grandeur of the trees
and substituted the towers of
insurance companies.

June 22, 1897, and Torontonians put on their finest and go out to admire the bunting celebrating the Diamond Jubilee of the great old queen. It's King St. East, looking east from Yonge St.

A great day for parades and loyal protestations: George V visits Toronto in 1901, and this extravagant archway, framing the Legislature, is erected to welcome him.

A Self-Sharpening Skate – Editor of The Star: Just returned from New York, and thinking of things seen and heard, etc., among which was a patent being applied for in a friend's office, a patent attorney. The application was for a self-sharpening skate – the more you skate the sharper they get. My friend the attorney said: "Although the self-contradicting expression was used, nevertheless it was an absolute, mechanical, positive fact." He, of course, could not reveal the particulars at present. What interested me more particularly was that the applicant was an old Toronto boy, born and raised here, his name is William Henry Haworth. Being introduced, I found him a fine, affable fellow. You can find the Canadian genius most anywhere. Old Boy. **The Star Feb. 2nd, 1914**

A Flim-Flam Game – The Old, Old Confidence Trick Successfully Operated On A Yonge Street Store Clerk To The Amount Of $10. – A youth employed in the store of Albert Britnell, 254 1-2 Yonge street, was flim-flammed out of $10 last evening by a gentlemanly-looking individual with a plausible manner.

The stranger called at the store, and producing a roll of $1 bills asked the boy give him a $10 bill for them, as he wanted to send it in a letter. The boy handed over two fives, but on counting over the ones he found only nine. The stranger took the fives and the ones, apparently sealed the fives in an envelope, and, handing it to the boy, walked out, remarking that he would be back with the other one in a moment.

The boy waited an hour and then opened the envelope. It was empty. **The Star August 2nd, 1898**

BEFORE THERE WAS A PEOPLE CITY, THERE WERE PEOPLE AND A CITY

One of the more arrogant assertions of modern Toronto is that it is People City–as if all that existed before was bricks and mortar. Of course, the politicians and media who mouth this platitude are trying to say that nowadays the city is for the people, instead of being dominated by commerce or industry.

Hmm.

Seems to me that cities are collections of people who live in bricks and mortar, mansions, highrises, mudhuts, what have you, and that the interesting thing is what kind of people make what kind of city.

Here are groups of people from Toronto's history, and most of them seemed to be having a good time.

Solemn occasion: April 23, 1842. A gathering in the prayer hall at Upper Canada College.

The Red Jacket Rink of the Toronto Curling Club poses on Toronto Bay in 1872. Their backs must have been stiff, because in those days a photo like this took 20 seconds or more to expose.

Nah then, wot's all this abaht, then! No, it's not a London bobby but a Toronto bobby–in 1875, complete with British police helmet that was still worn by Toronto police at the turn of the century. In fact, this kind of helmet went out mainly because of the introduction of police cars, whose low roofs forced the police to adopt flat caps.

Historically-minded members of the York pioneers group parade to the Toronto exhibition on August 22, 1879, to erect log cabins the way real pioneers did almost a century before.

Dr. Henry Scadding and friend contemplate, during the 1880s, the site of Castle Frank, a Grecian mansion built of logs by Governor John Graves Simcoe in the 1790s. It was acquired in 1808 by the Scadding family, but burned down in 1829. Dr. Scadding was one of the first of Canada's urban historians.

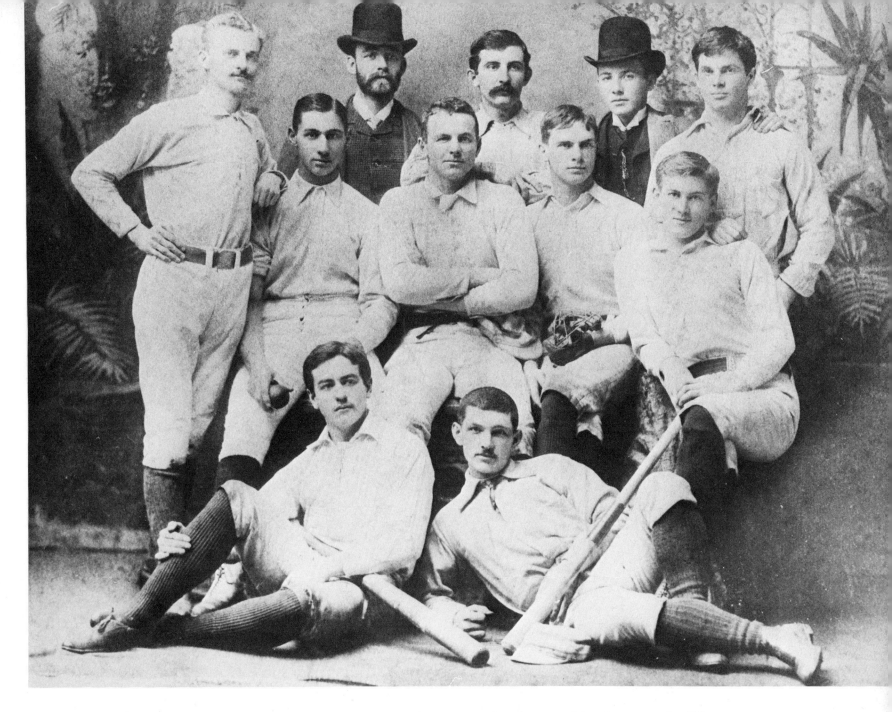

Ninety years ago, people actually participated in sports rather than watching them on color TV. Here's the University of Toronto's Varsity Base Ball Club in 1887.

The Toronto Snowshoe Club, made up of
members of the Toronto Lacrosse Club, face the
lens in front of a fountain at Queen's Park, at the
head of University Avenue, in the mid-1880s.

But in summer, there were the delights of cycling stylishly through the leafy streets of the growing metropolis, something that came back into style 80 years later. The Toronto Bicycle Club about 1890.

It seems hard to believe, but this photograph was taken on the farm of John Lawrence about 1895.
The farm was on what is now the northwest corner at Yonge Street and Lawrence Avenue.

Rather self-consciously, the people who made their business in Little York pose at the turn of the century. The photograph shows the north side of the Danforth, to the west of Dawes Road.

Something like Tom Brown's Schooldays, but a century or so later, the camera captures a students' fight from the YMCA building at the University of Toronto about 1902.

Mine host and helper. The bar of the Empringham Hotel on the Danforth, at the southwest corner of the Dawes Road intersection in the early 1900s. The owner, G.F. Empringham, is on the right.

Like something out of Dickens. Children at the East End Day Nursery on Dundas Street East in 1902. The nursery was on the north side of Dundas between Sackville and Sumach streets.

Was there ever such a splendid machine? It's 1906, and this tourer draws an admiring crowd
outside the King Edward Hotel on King Street East.

Gallant lads all! Fires devastated Toronto's downtown and its acres of wooden inner suburbs throughout much of its early history. Something of the pride of the men who fought the fires shows in this 1908 photograph of the East Toronto Fire Department at their firehall on Dawes Road, just north of the Danforth.

The wonders of technology! The Evening Telegram and the Toronto Star competed furiously to
get the news to the reader. Here the Telegram steals a march by projecting election results to a
crowd on Bay Street on the June 8, 1908, election night.

No bikinis then, but the pools were still jammed. The High Park Mineral Baths in 1911, from a postcard.

Immigrant women sweeping the sidewalk on the Danforth in the 1920s. The city was booming, but life was hard for many of its people.

The heart of the financial district, Canada's Wall Street—an organ grinder on Bay Street about 1922. In a few years, the stock market crash was going to make monkeys out of the Bay Street Barons who tossed the old man an occasional coin.

Before the masses could flee to Cottage Country by car, they used to take the streetcar instead to the relatively unpolluted lakeshore. Sunnyside in 1924.

A Peril To The Public – Whoever is responsible, whether the city or the railway companies, for the offensive condition of the slips at the foot of Brock street, the further continuance of such a nuisance is not only a disgrace, but a menace to the health of the citizens. Hundreds of people make their way, hurriedly, past this foul spot every evening to reach the boats for the Island. On the return journey however, coming from the fresh breezes of the Lake and Island, the sudden plunging into the foetid atmosphere surrounding Brock street wharf is almost enough to knock one backwards. If the City Engineer is powerless to act in the matter, he should report at once and the Council should in the interests of the public health, and the fair name of the city, do something to abate this crying nuisance. **The Star 1896**

THE PUBLIC PRIDE OF HOGTOWN THE GREAT

Something that has been constant throughout Toronto's history, to judge from historical books and files of old newspapers and magazines, has been the insistence that Toronto's system of government, public buildings, transportation, sewers, taxation operations, police, fire department and virtually anything to do with public life are absolutely unique–and the greatest.

One expression of this in recent times has been the boosterism and hucksterism of developers of suburban housing, or the media contentment with the "unique multicultural blend" in Toronto that was supposed to have no social frictions between different racial groups.

Sophisticated observers grate their teeth at this, but nevertheless throughout much of its history Toronto has seemed to generate a real civic pride. Some manifestations of this have been ludicrous–like the newspaper story that had "Old misty-eyed Metro" taking a girl lake swimmer to its heart a few years back. But the popular feeling of pride and interest in the girl was real enough.

It was the same a century ago. Torontonians insisted their public buildings had to be the best and that civic facilities had to work. One unfortunate aspect was that buildings that were being replaced were usually torn down. In the 1800s as well as the 1900s, life for quite substantial Toronto buildings could be a few decades. Compare this with Florence, which began equally commercially as a major Renaissance city. There the old palaces still stand in the centre of the city.

Of course, Toronto is still young, only two hundred years old. In five hundred years we may learn a little how to conserve.

So you thought toll gates were invented in modern times, to help pay for expressways? Yonge Street had a series of toll gates from 1820 to as late as 1894. They kept moving north as the city grew, taxing those who did business along the highway. They were leased by the year to gatekeepers, incredibly enough. In 1868, there were six tollgates, and the lessees paid sums ranging from $455 for one a mile and a half north of the town line to $5,000 or more for the gate at Yorkville. The gate pictured here was at Yonge and Cottingham, up from Bloor Street, an intersection that no longer exists.

This was Toronto's seventh main post office, built in 1852 on the west side of Toronto street, between King and Adelaide. Such was the growth of the city that it was too small in only 20 years. Miraculously, the building still stands, preserved from the wrecker by E.P. Taylor's Argus Corporation.

In 1873 this mansard-roofed building became Toronto's eighth post office. It stood on Adelaide at the head of Toronto Street. Nothing could save it from the devastation of progress.

The St. Lawrence Hall, once Toronto's town hall, in 1873. Its recent restoration has probably made the old building spiffier, and certainly costlier, than ever before.

44

The central prison on Strachan Avenue in 1884.

The old Union Station. Substantially more elegant than the current building, which also is one of an endangered species. Photo dates from 1885. It was built in 1873, pulled down 40 years later. The present Union Station has already lasted 50 per cent longer than its predecessor.

This was Upper Canada College in 1884, an elite school that stood at King and Simcoe from 1831 to 1891. It was an interesting spot then, with Upper Canada College on the northwest corner, a hotel across the street on the northeast, St. Andrew's Church on the southeast and Government House on the southwest. The corner was known as Education, Legislation, Salvation and Damnation.

Notorious or splendid, depending on whether you are a mental hospital reformer or an architect–999 Queen Street East. The dome and staircase became, a century later, a centre of conflict as the government wanted to pull it down and lovers of old buildings wanted to refurbish it. This picture was taken in 1884, before newer buildings cluttered up the frontage.

The Gay Nineties and the austere 1870s combine in this 1893 photo of a "tally-ho" bound for the annual Varsity games in Rosedale. The building is the Engineering block, erected in 1877.

Well, frivolity never did have much of a chance in old Toronto, or at least not in late-Victorian Toronto. This delightful concoction stood in Allan Gardens from 1878 to 1902. The land was donated by the Allans, one of old Toronto's great families, at a time when Jarvis Street was a place of sprawling estates and great houses.

Way down the street from the homes of the nobs, the St. Lawrence Market in the 1890s. By this time, there was a cigar factory in the formerly splendid St. Lawrence Hall, and the area smelled of horse dung, cabbages, and tobacco.

The old city hall of Toronto was the forum for civic development for 55 years at the southeast corner of Front and Jarvis, even though its white brick building was generally considered an eyesore. It was demolishd in 1899, a year after the opening of the new city hall at the head of downtown Bay Street.

R.T. Coady, city treasurer, in his office in 1898 before the transfer to the new city hall.

A staircase in the old city hall demolished in 1899. Photo was taken in 1898.

Spitting strictly prohibited, says a sign in this room in the city Courthouse, built in 1853 and demolished in 1900. Even the gasjets could hardly have made this room seem less utilitarian.

The great and the near-great gather on the steps of the new city hall for opening ceremonies on September 18, 1899. There was to be no longer the indignity of a brick building the American visitors sneered at. No one could have dreamed then that, less than 70 years later, a large body of citizens would want to tear down the new city hall because the city council had moved across the street to a building designed by a Finn in an international competition.

A view you can share with your grandparents. The facade of Osgoode Hall with the tower of the 1898 city hall, photographed in 1910. The scene is still the same. Osgoode Hall was begun in 1829. The iron fence that surrounds it was intended to keep out stray cattle, because it was going up in what was then farmland outside the city limits.

Another virtually unchanged scene. The library of Osgoode Hall, which is the headquarters of the Law Society of Upper Canada.

The newspaper reading room of the Toronto Public Library in 1900. The building, at Church and Adelaide, was originally the Mechanics Institute, an educational centre for the working class, and this room was the music hall. The institute turned over its assets to the city in 1883 for use as a public library.

Yorkville has bitten the dust as an independent municipality, and so has its town hall, shown here about 1907. It stood on the west side of Yonge Street, opposite Collier.

60

Impressive to a Torontonian is the fact that there was a public lavatory at Toronto Street and Adelaide at the turn of the century. Not as charming, perhaps, as the vespasians of Paris, but certainly more openly displayed than one could find public toilets in the Toronto of the second half of the century.

The Toronto General Hospital stood on the north side of Gerrard Street East from 1856 to 1913, between Sackville and Sumach. The buildings and grounds are gone, turned into a rather wretched area of housing and stores.

This gymnasium at the University of Toronto, interestingly functional in appearance, lasted from 1893 to 1912.

Firehall No. 1 stood at Bay and Temperance in 1912, singularly archaic in style for what was well on the way to becoming one of the world's major financial centres. Only eight years before, virtually the whole of the downtown had been reduced to ashes, and if this was the city's major firehall, one can understand why.

Convocation Hall at the University of Toronto, looking southwest, in 1925. Surprisingly, the view today is not that much different, apart from the fact that the highest freestanding structure in the world, the CN Tower, has been erected in the left distance.

The University of Toronto campus in 1920. Much is unchanged today. Have fun seeing what's new.

Good Times – Proof of Returning Prosperity Found In Two Busy Toronto Factories – "Hello! What's this?"

"This" was one evidence of returning good times, and of Toronto's foremost position in the big mercantile ranks. Eight large Canadian Pacific Railway drays, piled high with boxes, which bore this sign: "First shipment, 1898; Dunnett, Crean & Co., hat manufacturers, Balmuto street, Toronto," formed a procession, which attracted a great amount of attention today at noon, as they proceeded down Yonge street to the freight sheds.

The factory of the Gendron Bicycle Co. has begun to run night and day, turning out the '98 wheels as fast as it can be done. Between 500 and 600 men have been put at work. **The Star Jan. 5th, 1898**

THE HUB OF COMMERCE, MIGHTY ENGINE OF CANADA

Governor Simcoe planned York as a kind of cross between a mini-Athens and a garrison town. But the settlement just grew and grew, and with immigrants flooding in and the expansion of the railway system, the town that later became the city of Toronto became more and more a place to buy and sell and to make goods, rather than just a home for the rulers of a colony.

It was a tempestuous city, what with rebellions and riots in the first half of the century, and immigrant brawls and fires in the second half. But the stores and business offices, cattle markets and meat packing plants, the railway junctions and the port, the piano factories, the printers, all changed the frontier spirit of Toronto.

They were making steam engines in Toronto in 1833. In 1851, 2,600 persons were engaged in manufacturing and 204 of these were tailors and 384 made boots and shoes.

In 1871, there were 9,400 engaged in manufacturing. One rolling mill employed more than 300. There were 12,708 wage earners in 1871. This doubled in the next decade. In 1901, there were 45,515 wage earners. In 1871, 10.8 per cent of the province's manufacturing was done in Toronto, but by 1901 it was 34 per cent. Today, of course the labor force in metropolitan Toronto is over 1.5 million.

As a financial centre, Toronto grew slowly, because naturally the control of wealth was in the hands of the metropolis of Canada, Montreal. But by the turn of the century about one third of the bank branches in Western Canada were branches of Toronto banks, and the pendulum was swinging in Toronto's favour.

In the latter part of the 19th century, the opening up of the mines of northern Ontario created huge wealth in Toronto, which became the centre of trading in mineral stocks.

There can be no question but that after the opening of the transcontinental railways Toronto felt more and more the desire to outpace Montreal. This partly explains the size and attempts at splendour of many of the commercial buildings of late nineteenth century Toronto. Even if they couldn't rival many of the big Montreal enterprises, except in rate of growth, Toronto companies were determined to have imposing offices. It was a case of No. 2 trying harder. Now that Toronto is definitely No. 1 in size and wealth, will the city take a breather?

How very, very commercial. Downtown in 1861, looking northwest from the south side of Adelaide Street, east of Victoria Street.

You could get away from the hustle and bustle of the great city in the 1870s by taking an ice boat over to Centre Island and quaffing a few at the hotel owned by Mrs. Emily Parkson. The pub under new management was still going strong forty years later. The harbour froze over completely in those days, before the ferry boats acted as icebreakers.

In 1872, the Canada Marble Works of Robert Forsyth made funeral monuments for deceased Torontonians on King Street West, between Bay and York. It was No. 80 King West, later the site of the Toronto Star building and now of the Bank Of Montreal's giant white skyscraper.

King Street West, from Bay to
Simcoe Streets, in the 1870s.
The fine building in the left
foreground was the United
Empire Club.

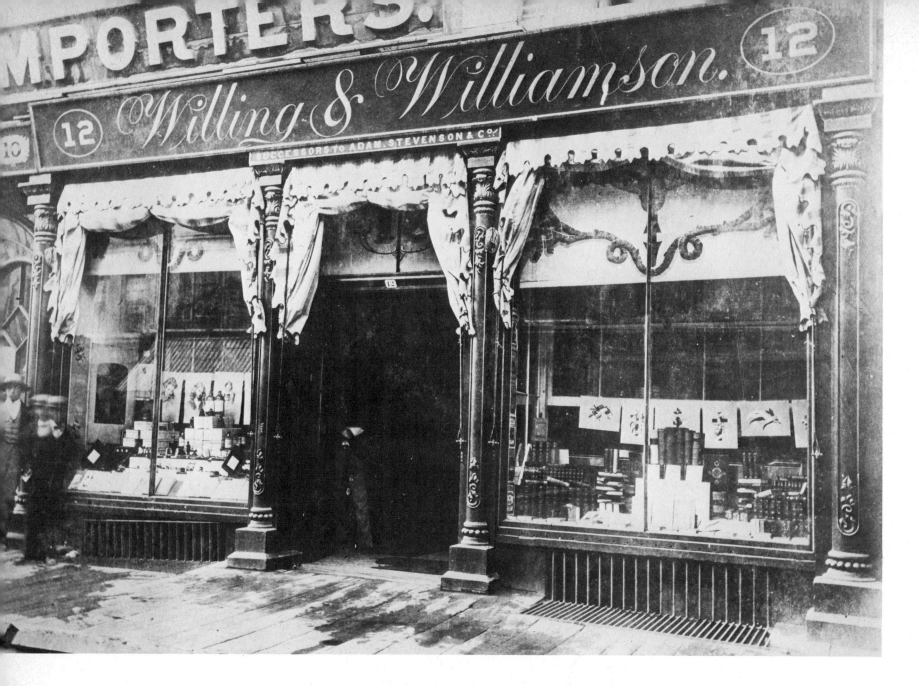

A classy bookstore of the 1870s, Willing and Williamson, on King St. East between Yonge and Victoria, roughly across the street from where the King Edward Hotel now stands, itself a piece of *fin de siecle* grandeur.

This was the metropolis: looking along Front Street from Yonge to Jarvis. The big building in the background was the much-criticized white brick City Hall (1844-99) that was abandoned in 1898 for the grandiose new City Hall, in turn abandoned in the 1960s for the flying saucer and clamshell design of Viljo Revell.

Yonge Street, west side, south of King Street about 1880. The Bank of Montreal (1845-1885) and the Custom House (1876-1919). As the meagre life spans of these quite presentable buildings show, Toronto aways was one of the wreckingest of cities.

This was the Bank of Upper Canada on King Street East when that noteworthy financial institution was founded in 1822. The bank, and with it a lot of fortunes, crashed in 1866, but the old building was still there in 1885.

When Front Street was elegant rather than commercial: the Queen's hotel, between Bay and York Street, in 1886. The mammoth Royal York stands on spot today. The trees, of course, were rooted out long, long ago.

The very latest in shopping convenience–the Yonge Street Arcade in 1885. It was a forerunner of Toronto's modern buried downtown malls, most grandiose of which is the Eaton Centre. Somewhere in the 1920s, this good idea got lost for close to 50 years.

The coffin block, they called it, in the core between Front and Wellington Streets East. The picture was taken about 1885. Most of the buildings have been devastated, though a few remain. The knell of progress tolled slowly in this part of the city, once one of the busiest.

A fine commercial hotel, the American, stood on the northeast corner of Front and Yonge. Photo about 1888.

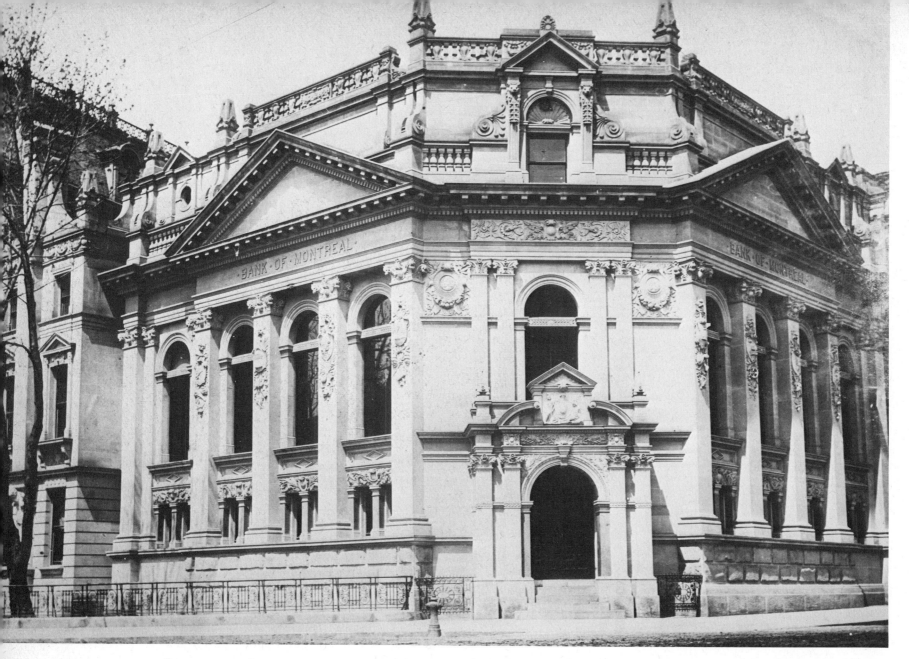

Some extraordinary guidance from above has preserved this Bank of Montreal building, opened 1886, on the northwest corner of Yonge and Front. A few ugly clocks and signs have been added, but in essence this is the same heavily ornamented building your grandfather admired. The photo was taken about 1890, but you, dear reader, can walk up to and walk into this stylish temple of commerce, goggle at the stained glass skylights and start to mourn what has gone irretrievably.

One-horsepower streetcar on Spadina Avenue in the 1890s. Today's Spadina subway has
massive displays of public art, but can never quite capture the intimacy customers on this older
type of transport shared.

Monumental but ugly: the
Confederation Life Building on the
north side of Richmond between
Yonge and Victoria streets. This brutal
architecture is no doubt meant to
evoke the chateaux of France, but
lacks the grace even the Normans
managed to put into their keeps.

York Street, looking north from south of King Street in the 1890s. A well known hotel, the Rossin House, is on the right. This was a rather aging area, and its buildings showed a more gentle style than that of the more ambitious, and often ugly, buildings going up to the east.

This sturdy building was the Agricultural Hall, which stood on the northwest corner of Yonge and Queen about 1870.

The Telegram building that stood on the southwest corner of the King and Bay from 1879 to 1900.
After that, the Telegram moved to Bay and Melinda, then to Front Street W., and then to oblivion.

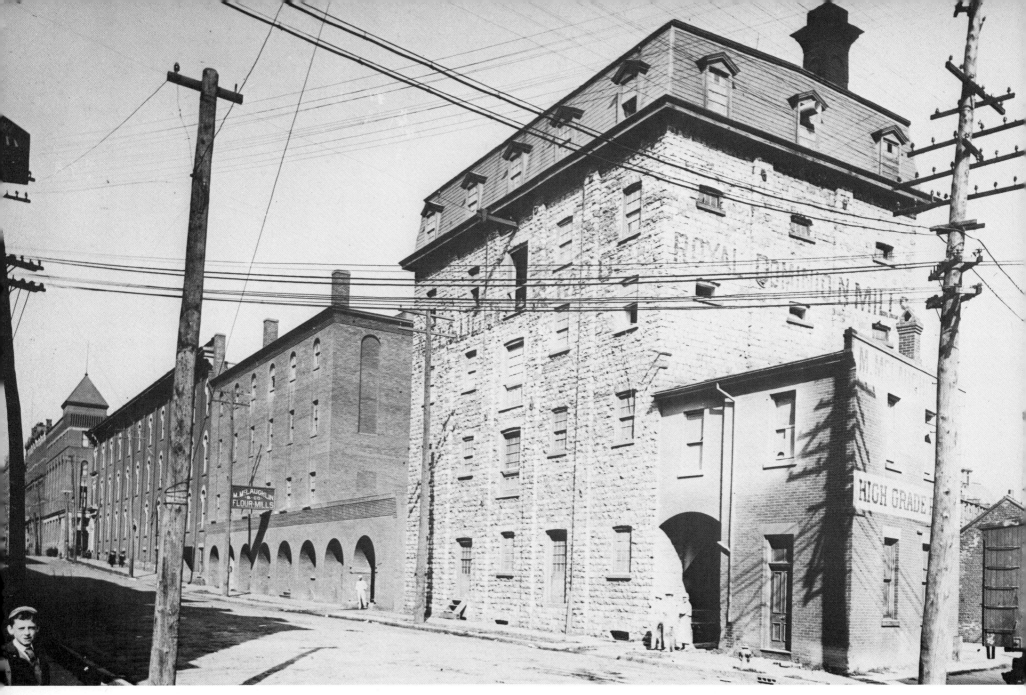

McLaughlin and Co.'s flour mill stood at the turn of the century on the east side of Bay Street, from the Esplanade to north of Front St. This grim establishment at the foot of the Wall Street of Canada was replaced by undistinguished government architecture.

No doubt of it, they bred drivers hardier in the old days. A delivery truck for the T. Eaton
Company in the early 1900s.

That Telegram building at Bay and Melinda, opened in 1900, contained this reception room on its editorial floor.

At the foot of the town were the docks, and even in 1906 at many of the berths were still sailing ships.

Yonge and Bloor is today the hub of
the Mile of Mink, and vast buildings
tower over the subway junction. But
in the early 1900s, when this building
was coming down on the southeast
corner of the intersection, large scale
development was just starting.

Pride of ownership: Rutherford's Cut Rate Drug Store on Spadina, at the northwest corner of the Nassau St. intersection, just before the Great War.

Inside Rutherford's Drugs: photographic evidence that old drug stores really did look the way they do in Norman Rockwell paintings.

Before the TTC there was the Toronto Railway Company. Here are its streetcar barns on Yorkville Avenue between Yonge and Bay, about 1912.

Court Street about 1912: the parking was free and easy.

The Toronto Transportation Commission was founded in 1920 to amalgamate all of the city's buses and streetcars under public ownership. It was one of the pioneers of this concept, and London Transport, for example, is no older than the TTC. Here's one of the TTC bus fleet, on Glen Road, Rosedale in 1923.

One thing the angular new skyscrapers that went up on the eve of the Depression couldn't remove was the grace of the passenger steamers that still plied the Great Lakes. The Canada Steamship Lines passenger terminals about 1930.

Huzzah! The pride of Toronto in the post-World War I and pre-World War II era was the Canadian National Exhibition. It seemed to feature on every newsreel of the era, along with the ballroom of the Royal York. The Dufferin Gate, pictured in all its glory in the 1920s, captures some of that pizzaz–which had become a rare commodity as legislation against booze and the growing spirit of the Toronto Sunday, coupled with the demolition of much of the downtown during the Tremendous (early) Twenties, had robbed the city of much of its former elegance and visual vigour.

A Boom For The West – Vast Immigration Coming – In Ten Years The Balance Of Population Will Be West Of Lake Superior – The loss of good Canadian brawn and blood and brain to the States is about stopped; the flood is beginning to come this way.

This is the sum of the opinions of men who are in the place to know, and their judgment is corroborated by that of every observer, expert or casual, of the present trend of migration on this continent.

"The emigration of Canadians to the States has ceased," said W. D. Scott, of the Manitoba Emigration Office at York and Front streets, this morning. "A few years ago we had to work pretty hard to overcome the popular tendency to seek the States. Now we have practically dismissed it from our calculations. There is, of course, one thing to be borne in mind: the farming lands of the States have been all taken up, and there are few places where a settler may go.

Some We Do Not Want – But that's not the only point. There are thousands of farmers in the North-western States who would be glad to come to Canada if we would offer any inducements. But we are not anxious to have them. Their minds are filled up with fake politics. They are called Populists in their own country. They do not make good settlers. They seldom stay in one place for any great time, and are constantly roaming about.

"No," said Mr. Scott, reflectively, "we don't want any galvanized Americans, but we are going to get thousands of the best people of the United States before very long." **The Globe & Mail Jan. 24th, 1898**

SOLDIERS OF THE QUEEN, MORE BRITISH THAN THE BRITONS

Sometimes in Toronto it seems hard to imagine that the wars and the destruction that afflict the rest of the world could ever involve this peaceful city.

But Toronto was founded mainly as a military base and was the site of a major battle in its infancy. (A battle that the local team lost.)

The Americans took Fort York in 1812 and burned the town down.

Soldiers were sent from Toronto to subdue the rebellious Metis in the North West Rebellion.

Troops from Toronto fought the Boers in the South African War. And, of course, the city was a major producer both of men and munitions for World War I and World War II, while Torontonians died in Korea and still stand on guard in such outlandish places as Cyprus and the Middle East.

Officers of the British 30th Regiment
ham it up for the camera in front of the
Parliament Buildings on Front St. W.
in 1861.

A famous photo, this: veterans of the War of 1812 attend a garden party of the Fifth Militia District Rifle Association on the grounds of the ''Rosedale'' mansion on October 23, 1861.

A picture that shows the good old days were not quite so spruced up as the bad old present: the Western Gate of Fort York in 1885. Now it has become Old Fort York, heavily reconstructed, with the roar of expressway traffic perhaps louder than the cannonfire when the Americans stormed the place in 1812.

July 23, 1885: Men of the Queen's Own Rifles returning in triumph from suppressing the North West Rebellion at the CPR's North Toronto station.

Hail the conquering heroes come–from putting down the Boers. Troops returning from the South African War march down Bay Street.

Presumably it's Warrior's Day at the Canadian National Exhibition, as this martial group parades
King Street East in 1906.

Off to the slaughter. Cavalry parade along Bloor
Street before leaving for the Great War in 1915.

105

Sir Robert Borden inspects Royal Air Force men at the University of Toronto during the First World War.

The Armouries, 1891-1963. RIP. This symbol of Toronto's military heritage was pulled down to make room for the Ontario Supreme Court Building on University Avenue, after a battle of words fully as bitter as any passage of arms.

Policeman's Bible Class — A class consisting of members of the police force is in the habit of meeting weekly on Tuesdays in one of the parlours of Shaftesbury Hall for bible study and intercourse. The meeting held yesterday afternoon was conducted by Rev. H.M. Parsons, of Knox Church, who was so pleased at the large attendance and great interest manifested, that he will take the class again next week. Although this class is conducted mainly in the interests of the police, of whom 50 belong to it, Christian workers of all kinds are heartily welcomed at its meetings, as its object is not only to do good among the members of the force, but to secure the sympathy and co-operation of the public. At the close of yesterday's studies the regular business meeting took place, when Sergeant Stephens was elected leader of the class, and Constable Frank Robinson secretary for the ensuing month. **The Globe & Mail March 25th, 1885**

TORONTO THE GOOD, CITY OF CHURCHES

Everybody has heard of Toronto the good, where the only thing to do on a Sunday was to go to church. That era seems long gone, although in fact "open" Sunday, with sports and movie theatres and booze at restaurants, dates only from the 1960s.

But most of the churches remain, although quite a number have been demolished. The best way to see the churches of Toronto is to go and see the buildings themselves.

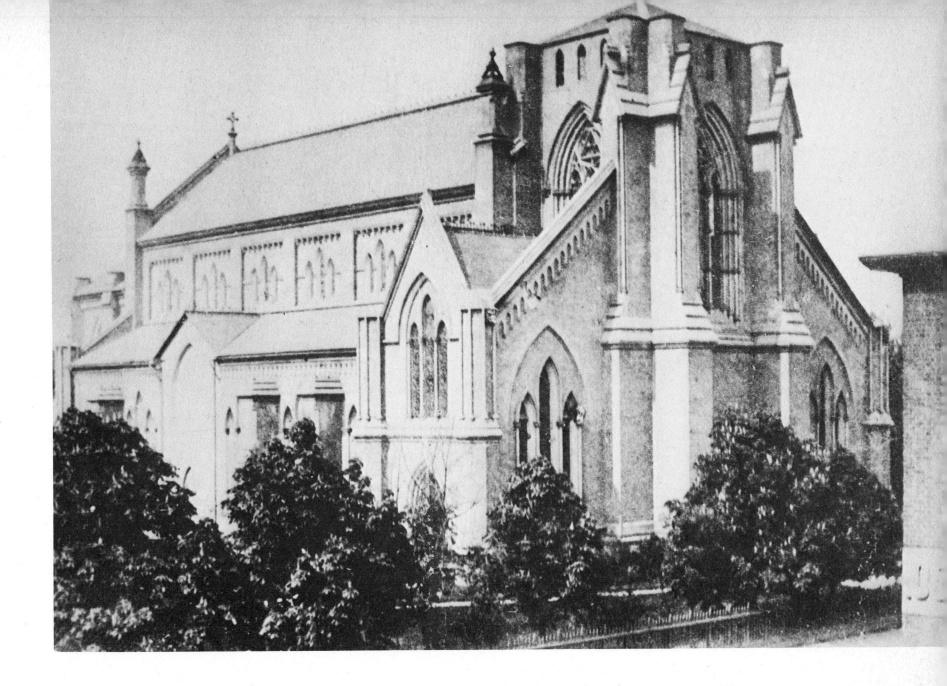

St. James Cathedral without its spire in 1859. It was six years old at the time.

The Church of the Holy Trinity as it was in 1908 when Eaton's warehouses were under construction. Now the warehouses are gone, Holy Trinity remains, and a new Eaton's complex surrounds the church, built in 1847.

Metropolitan United Church—or as it was when photographed in the 1870s, soon after completion, Metropolitan Methodist.

Deer Park Presbyterian Church, opened in 1890, when this picture was taken.

The sensuous sweep of the seating at Trinity United Church (formerly Methodist) on Bloor Street West, was photographed about 1910. The dour exterior of this massive, blocky building gives little hint of the interior glories.

One hundred years after the first churches of Toronto were founded, St. John the Baptist Anglican out on Kingston Road was still an affair of logs. The picture was taken in 1919.

A gentleman who had recently come to the city from the United States says that one marked feature of business life in this city is the late hour at which business begins in the morning. Whereas, in American cities stores are open at half-past seven or eight, and businessmen are in their offices and ready for business by nine o'clock at latest, here the largest stores open leisurely about nine o'clock, and a business man cannot be seen on business until about ten o'clock. The gentleman in question seemed to think this a fault, but considering that Toronto does at least as much business as any American city of equal size, the argument would seem to show that one reason why Toronto businessmen do not work so hard as Americans is, to use the current slang, "because they don't have to." **Globe & Mail Jan. 9th, 1888**

The growth and development of the West End has been remarkable...The East End will emulate the West End. Act Now. Terms are easy. One dollar down four dollars when you sign your agreement or see the property – it is optional – the balance you can pay five dollars monthly for thee years. Don't wait until spring when prices will advance. There are not many homesites to be disposed of. **Dawes Road property ad. 1914**

THE RIGHT SIDE OF THE TRACKS

The houses of the rich in old Toronto were enormous. You couldn't afford to build that way today, even if you could afford to buy such large plots of land in the central city. Of course, even the rich can't afford to live in houses of the size their grandparents lived in these days, because of the invention of income tax. That helps explain how such a small city as Toronto was, when many of the large houses pictured in this section were built, could have such rich people. The social structure funneled the wealth produced in the area into a few hands, and the government didn't take it away from them to redistribute the wealth. But for those who live in small apartments in multi-storey apartments today–look and weep.

George Templeman Kingston's home on Queen's Park Crescent West, about 1888. It's now the site of the University of Toronto Medical Building.

Now this was living with style: Moss Park, the mansion that stood on the west side of Sherbourne Street. Picture was taken about 1897. All that's left now is the name of a housing project.

The library of Moss Park, after it had become a museum. Originally it was the dining room. Photo taken in 1896.

James Austin's home, Spadina, on Spadina Road opposite Austin Terrace, in the 1880s.

Sir James Buchanan Macaulay's massive Wykeham Hall stood on the south side of College Street, east of Bay Street, where Eatons were later to build a store that was itself largely to succumb in 1977. The house is pictured abut 1915. It was used as the Bishop Strachan School from 1870 to 1915.

The drawing room of Wykeham Hall, College Street, about 1915.

William Warren Baldwin's mansion on the north east corner of Bay and Front, about 1885.

Henry John Boulton, one of the Family Compact, built Holland House, which stood on the south side of Wellington Street between Bay and York streets. This is a rear view of the massive home, taken in 1904.

Lawyer D'Arcy Boulton built the Grange in 1820 – and it still stands behind the Art Gallery of Ontario, a museum of old Toronto. Pictured here in the 1890's.

William Cawthra's mansion stood on the northeast corner of Bay and King when it was photographed in 1897. By that time it had become The Molsons Bank. Today the Bank of Nova Scotia building occupies site.

Sir William Mortimer Clark and his family pose for the camera about 1912, in the drawing room of their home on Wellington Street West, near Clarence Street.

The Clarks lived in style. This was another view of their drawing room.

Beverley House stood on the northeast corner of Richmond and John streets. The photo is from 1911.
The house was built by Sir John Beverley Robinson.

The dining room of Beverley House.

Simeon H. Janes' little place in the suburbs was Benvenuto, on the west side of Avenue Road, south of Edmund Avenue. This picture, from the 1890s, shows the gatehouse.

Inside Benvenuto, the style of living was what you might expect in a European chateau. This was the dining room.

Toronto Gets Better Terms On New Loan – City Treasurer Doesn't Quite Understand Cable Message, But Says It Is Good News

London, Feb. 6 – A new half million sterling loan for Toronto in 4½ at 99 is being arranged. Toronto's last loan, which was at 97½ is now quoted at $7 for the $2½ paid, which is equivalent to 101½.

City Treasurer Coady and his deputy, Mr. Patterson, stated to The Star that they could not quite understand the meaning of the cable. The last sentence apparently refers to the debenture issue hypothecated by Lloyd's Bank to meet the loan which matures in August.

"Fifty per cent of this issue was not sold by the bank, and it has been carried by them," said Mr. Patterson. "The price they have now obtained is above par, but of course they have been paying interest charges for two months."

Mr. Patterson stated that the price obtained showed that money is now considerably cheaper and that the city's credit is good. **The Star Feb. 6th, 1914**

AFTER PRIDE – AN INFERNO, THEN MORE PRIDE ...

The city of Toronto several times has built anew after much of the important part of the town has been reduced to ashes. In 1849, up to 15 acres of the heart of the town was burned down, including the old St. James Cathedral. The blaze reportedly could be seen from 50 miles away.

But Toronto sprang back quickly.

The fire at University College in 1890 shows how quick recovery can be. A servant stumbled on the stairs–he was carring a tray of kerosene lamps. They fell and the blaze engulfed the building, destroying the east wing and the library.

In a few years all was restored–and expanded.

The Great Fire of 1904 ruined a dozen blocks downtown. The damage pictures are still spectacular, even to a world grown familiar with blitzed cities.

Yet by the time the boom of the early 1920s was in full swing, who would have believed there had ever been anything else but the towers that were rising. For what had been burned in 1904 was buildings–not the confidence and wealth of Toronto.

The University College under construction, 1857.

University College after the fire of February, 1890.

The restored University College, 1907.

The Library of University College, 1884.

After the Great Fire of Toronto–April 27, 1904. Front Street, looking west from the top of the Customs House on Yonge Street. That's right, the whole business district, most of which was new, has been burned out as thoroughly as if it had been blitzed.

A fire next to the Toronto Telegram on May 9, 1905, in a mattress factory is doused by the Telegram's fire equipment. The smoke and flames have been heavily touched up, no doubt to acquaint the reader with the awesome battle the newspaper had to put up to beat the flames.

The west side of Bay Street, looking south from Melinda, 1904.

Downtown Toronto 20 years after the great fire—
in 1924. The phoenix city has sprung up again,
and we can be sure the people of the time were
convinced there could never be anything bigger
and better than what they had built. Of course,
these buildings have been replaced with bigger
ones, sometimes 60 storeys bigger. But better?
Perhaps we have to wait and see what our
grandchildren have to say.